Meditations for Cats Who Do Too Much

Learning to Take Things One Life at a Time

PENGUIN BOOKS

Meditations for Cats Who Do Too Much

Michael Cader

illustrations by Peter Spacek

PENGUIN BOOKS
Published by the Penguin Group
Penguin Books USA Inc., 375 Hudson Street, New York,
New York 10014, U.S.A.
Penguin Books Ltd, 27 Wrights Lane,
London W8 5TZ, England
Penguin Books Australia Ltd, Ringwood, Victoria, Australia
Penguin Books Canada Ltd, 10 Alcorn Avenue, Toronto,
Ontario, Canada M4V 3B2
Penguin Books (N.Z.) Ltd, 182–190 Wairau Road,
Auckland 10, New Zealand

Penguin Books Ltd, Registered Offices: Harmondsworth,
Middlesex, England

First published in Penguin Books 1993
1 3 5 7 9 10 8 6 4 2
Copyright © Cader Company, Inc., 1993
Illustrations copyright © Peter Spacek and Cader Company,
Inc., 1993
All rights reserved

LIBRARY OF CONGRESS CATALOGING IN PUBLICATION DATA
Cader, Michael, 1961–
Meditations for cats who do too much: learning to take things
one life at a time/Michael Cader; illustrations by Peter Spacek.
p. cm.
ISBN 0 14 01.7799 X
1. Cats—Humor. 2. Psychology—Humor. I. Title.
PN6231.C23C33 1993
818'.5402—dc20 92–38347

Printed in the United States of America
Set in Bodoni Book
Designed by Kathryn Parise

Dedication

To Herschel, Cinnabar, Chutney, Truffles,
Dr. Nut, and Lydia, for their invaluable help, research,
and inspiration. And to Amos, a shining
example of the other side.

Dedication

To Herschel, Cinnabar, Chutney, Truffles,
Dr. Nut, and Lydia, for their invaluable help, research,
and inspiration. And to Amos, a shining
example of the other side.

The 9-Life Recovery Program

1. *Admitting* that there is too much to be done, and I don't have to be the only cat in the world to do everything

2. *Accepting* the Higher Power (also known as The Owner) as my caretaker

3. *Praying* that the Higher Power comes back from that weekend at the beach

4. *Hoping* that the Higher Power believes I destroyed the closet in her absence out of love and loneliness, not anger

5. *Realizing* that I do not have to be the Higher Power's sole source of happiness and joy

6. *Acknowledging* that just because my food smells funny and I refuse to eat for three days doesn't mean that I have an eating problem

7. *Resolving* to do what I can do well, and then take a nap

8. *Allowing* myself to take another nap if I need to (or if there is nothing to chase)

9. *Taking* things one life at a time

Acknowledgments

Today we practically take the 9-Life Recovery Program for granted, but things were not always so. Our movement owes a large debt of gratitude to Lori L., who first recognized the need for cats to come together to share their problems and demanded that the Program proceed in the face of any obstacle.

The strength of her idea is demonstrated by its early and swift acceptance by both cats *and* penguins, who humbly reached across the division of species to help. And help they did, particularly Nicole G., Marsha B., and Michael J.—and many others still too early in their recovery to face public recognition.

From the professional community, Dr. Lisa Lebowitz provided invaluable counsel to the author in the course of shaping the ideas you are about to read. Her associate Dr. Seth often labors in the background, far from the urban chaos in which this program was fostered, but his help and support provide the foundation that makes such progress possible. Peter S. supplied his special karma to illustrating these ideas.

And a special thanks is owed to Jonathon L., who selflessly repressed his own agenda in favor of the greater good of the feline community. We wish him well in his own continuing struggle.

Contents

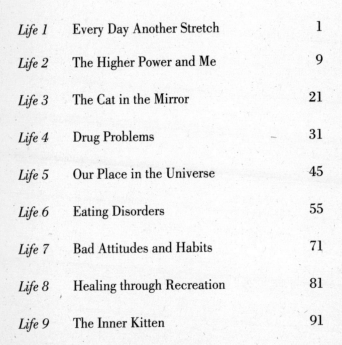

Introduction

As America's favorite household pet, cats are showered with attention, both at home and in the media. We are prized for our affectionate independence, our quiet and gentle manner, our heartfelt warmth, and our delicate features. And we have been the stars of many a book, both celebratory and humorous. And all of this attention is justly deserved.

But this newfound celebrity obscures a darker, sadder story. The pressure of being a Supercat is intense. The expectations are almost unrealistically high, the demands increasing, and there is so much to do. The ugly truth is that cats have problems, too. Let's say that again, all together this time, because just saying it out loud is very healthy: Cats have problems, too! Driven by the pressure of success and the need to keep up, cats nationwide have slowly and silently become napaholics, scratchaholics, and worst of all, shedaholics.

There has been evidence of eating disorders, attention problems, chronic fatigue, obsessive cleaning, indifference, and much more. And all the while, the Higher Powers that be have looked straight past these obvious warning signs, assuming this clearly abnormal behavior to be another one of the cat population's many charms—instead of its most deep-seated problem.

But finally cats are coming out of the closet (and from under the bed) to share our secret burdens with one another. We are joining support groups, meowing our hearts out, and licking fellow cats and their problems all at the same time. Of course, those codependent owners may need a little more time, since they have yet to admit their need to be needed by their cats. But that's another book altogether.

As we all know by now, the first step in overcoming any addictive problem is to admit that the problem exists. If *Meditations for Cats Who Do Too Much* accomplishes that and nothing else, it will have been worth the effort.

For napaholics, scratchaholics, and shedaholics alike—and for all cats who constantly struggle with the busy pressures of every day, the need to keep up, the juggling of both work and leisure in the same home with rarely a respite—*Meditations for Cats Who Do Too Much* offers comfort, thoughts, meditations, and answers.

While it is true that this book is written with cats specifically in mind, it is worth noting that numerous dogs have read the manuscript and found it very relevant to their lives as well. But this book is created by and for cats, and it is about our uniquely busy and pressure-filled lives.

Working on the premise that most cats are workaholics of one form or another, and therefore don't have time to read an entire year's worth of meditations, I've limited the book to a manageable number, to be used and enjoyed whenever time allows. The program is based around the 9-Life Recovery Program, widely accepted as the best self-healing method available for cats. The Nine Lives are our touchstones, the guiding posts that will lead us to a healthy, happy, productive, and balanced life-style, life after life. In keeping with the spirit of the program, the book will also include the occasional break for a nap, a snack, or chasing some lint.

Meditations for Cats Who Do Too Much

Life 1
Every Day Another Stretch

Admitting that there is too much to be done,
and I don't have to be the only cat in the
world to do everything

Awakening

"There will be no quote today, not until I am alert enough to appreciate it for what it is."

—The Author

A cat spends more time waking up than almost any other mammal because of its unique sleeping cycle. It takes great courage to face the dawn of a new day at least twelve times each day. This may explain why cats are given nine lives when lesser creatures are given only one.

Think of the bear, giant and ferocious, awesome in size and speed—well of course, because he has to awaken but once a year, and can thus devote his energies elsewhere. The cat is awakening constantly.

I will awaken at my own pace. I will stretch until limber. I will not be rushed.

The Struggle for Consciousness
(Awakening—Part 2)

"A cat has absolute emotional honesty: human beings, for one reason or another, may hide their feelings, but a cat does not."

—Ernest Hemingway

I like to hide many things, it is true—all of my cat toys, every pencil in the house, balls of fluff, the Higher Power's favorite slippers—but not my feelings. This is something that I know about myself, with a clarity as strong as my third eye.

I am what I am. I accept me. I embrace me. I search for my essential me-ness. I examine my every paw and I lick my fur, unremittingly. I . . . oh excuse me, is there someone else in the room?

I will emerge from the primordial closet and show my fur to the world. No staring, please.

Chasing Your Own Tail

"The tail in cats is the principal organ of emotional expression."

—Aldous Huxley

Indeed, our tails are the heart that we wear on our sleeves (if we had sleeves). It is our bellwether, our companion, our silent voice to the world. It is hard for a cat not to be fascinated by the many aspects of its tail.

And it is equally hard not to be proud of our remarkable speed and agility. But we have to remember that we do ourselves a disservice when we turn our talents on ourselves.

Chasing our tails is a daily problem, but it is also a metaphor for all of our problems. It seems inconceivable that the tail that dangles so close cannot be caught. And it seems inconceivable that goals that lie so close can be so hard to attain. But the more time we spend chasing our tails, the less time there is to chase our goals.

Today I will try really hard to remember that the tail that looks so tempting is my own, and I have already caught it.

Napaholism

"I never heard of one who suffered from insomnia."
—*Joseph Wood Krutch*

It's easy to make jokes about cats and sleep. But then it is always easier to laugh about a serious problem rather than confront it head on. Isn't it strange that the Higher Power always marvels at how often we sleep, but never questions whether it is normal?

Let sleeping cats lie, they say. But is it for our consideration or theirs? It is true, cats spend more time sleeping than nearly every other creature known to man. But it is also true that when we are active we exert tremendous amounts of energy relative to our body size.

There are indeed some cats with sleeping disorders, however. We can get so accustomed to regular resting that we forget the need to be awake occasionally as well. The napaholic sleeps through meals, neglects to wake the Higher Power before 6:00 A.M., and will sleep in any chair, whether sunny or shaded. Heed these warning signs and seek help if necessary. But don't wear yourself out with worry.

I recognize that napaholism is a serious, albeit rare, problem. I will reflect on my own habits. In fact, I think I will sleep on it.

Working at Home

"Dogs come when they are called; cats take a message and get back to you."

—Mary Bly

Long before technology made working at home in vogue for human beings, cats had smoothly adjusted to conducting both their business and their personal lives from the same dwelling.

Since we are not allowed anywhere *near* the computer when the plastic cover is off, even though it makes a dandy heater, we don't have an easy signal that indicates when we are working. And so we don't receive the respect that other domestic (home–office) workers now enjoy.

As the notion of "housewife" has changed, we can only hope "housecat" changes as well. Our days are indeed long, and the level of appreciation short. There is furniture to be sat on, toys to be hidden, litter to be rearranged, birds to be watched, affection to be granted, and much much more.

The key to a successful home office is establishing boundaries. Try to structure a regular workday for yourself, and take time for regular naps so that you can bring your best to bear, every day.

I am not a housecat, I am a domestic animal.

Conflict (Cat Fights)

> *"No matter how much cats fight, there always seem to be plenty of kittens."*
>
> —*Abraham Lincoln*

"Cat fight" is one of those unfortunate pejoratives that have worked their way into the language. Thank goodness Honest Abe set the record straight for us. Cats are fundamentally loving creatures, as clearly evidenced by our prodigious breeding capabilities.

The normal cat is incapable of such human foibles as holding a grudge or pursuing nuisance litigation for years on end. Yes, we do fight occasionally. And yes, there sometimes is a bit of bloodcurdling screeching and yowling. And maybe once in a great while someone gets scratched.

But is that so bad? We need to release our anger, and while fighting is not a way of life it can be the proper response when someone else is stealing your food. Since cats do not bottle up emotions, their fights rarely last very long and on balance are calmer than the squabbles of most other animals, including the Higher Power.

I am a peace-loving creature, but just because I am domesticated doesn't mean I'm a wimp.

Life 2
The Higher Power and Me

Accepting the Higher Power
(also known as The Owner)
as my caretaker

Fear When the Higher Power Leaves for the Weekend and You Are All Alone

"There are no illegitimate children—only illegitimate parents."

—Leon Yankwich

Abandonment is something we all face, from the day early in life when we are torn from our mothers and sent to a new home onward. (Many of us have never even *known* our real fathers.) And so every time the Higher Power prepares to leave, even for a short time, that feeling of abandonment is naturally triggered.

It is hard not to take it personally, not to think that it is something that we have done, or haven't done, or should have done. Did I shed too much? Should I have paid her a little more attention? Is my litter box untidy? Doesn't she know that sleeping on her face is a sign of love?

These kinds of questions are just so much stinkin' thinkin'. The simple truth is that the Higher Power ranges farther and wider than we are allowed, and that sometimes she is called away. The loss is hers for being absent from our presence.

It is not I that have driven the Higher Power away. I remain secure and rooted—in her bed.

Fear That the Higher Power Really Isn't Coming Back This Time

"Watch a cat when it enters the room for the first time. It searches and smells about. . . . It trusts nothing until it has examined . . . everything."

—Jean–Jacques Rousseau

I know, I just explained it. It's not your fault that the Higher Power is leaving, and it's only temporary. But what if this time is different? What if she really isn't coming back? What if I am not just feeling abandoned, but truly am being abandoned? Doesn't the *Enquirer* have articles like this all the time? Maybe I should plant myself in her suitcase, so that she knows she can't get away with this.

Whoa! Hold on there. Insecurity is one thing; insanity another. There's extra food in the bowl, and the cat-sitter should be here before sundown. The Higher Power *is* coming back, and you *are* going to make her pay the price. For now, enjoy the freedom (and if you get lonely, rearrange all of the shoes in her closet).

I need to conceal my need to be needed, so that the Higher Power will need me more. When she returns, I will play it cool.

13

Fear That the Higher Power Will Not Have Breakfast Ready by 5:30

"A recent census taken among cats shows that approximately 100 percent are neurotic. That estimate is probably on the low side."

—Stephen Baker

Do people really find this funny? Locked in the same house for our entire lives, expected to live up to a certain image of the Supercat, constantly being asked to play the stupid Shoelace Game (with conviction, no less!), and our reward is to be branded neurotic?

The earliest dawn is a time of great trepidation, and hunger is the most awesome force that drives us all. When people first came to this country, they had no qualms about rising at sunset and searching for food, for that was their life's mission. Couldn't we use a bit of that pioneering spirit again, that appreciation for the essentials of life? The Higher Power is capricious and unreliable while the stomach is constant. You can resist the force of nature, but you cannot disobey it.

My rational side knows that I will get fed eventually. My irrational side would like you to wake up and fill the damn bowl NOW.

Fear That the Higher Power Has Bought the Wrong Kind of Litter

"The cat obeys the Scriptures: 'Put not thy trust in things.' The cat is like the wise man: he trusts a principle; not a man of principle."

—Melvin B. Tolson

I know that flexibility is important to getting by life's little hurdles. But I also know that we must have our standards, that in certain matters flexibility is insufficient.

One of the constant risks of being a cat is the ever-changing status of the litter box. Every day can bring a new surprise, and a completely different state of affairs. The Higher Power seems to find this amusing, rather than a shameful lapse of constancy. But imagine if every time a human went into the bathroom the toilet was made of a completely different material, or had an entirely different smell—or had inadvertently been moved to a completely different part of the room.

To the Higher Power, litter may be a nuisance. But to me, litter is something that I count on. I will try to be flexible about my less important needs, if you will

simply bring home the premium brand instead of buy-
ing whatever is on sale.

*I will put my faith in the constancy of the litter, and if
that fails, I will use the nice white bathtub.*

Catnap:

*Take a minute to stop and eat the flowers. (Indoor cats
can substitute houseplants.)*

Fear That the Higher Power Likes Humans Better Than You

"If man could be crossed with the cat it would improve man, but it would deteriorate the cat."

—Mark Twain

Don't I spend hours and hours meticulously grooming myself every day? Don't I play silly games, pose fetchingly on the couch, chase birds through the window, rub against people's legs, and generally provide hours of entertainment and warmth—all without ever asking for an allowance or borrowing the car?

I'm cute, I'm clean, I'm warm, I'm even economical—and I am descended from Asian royalty. So why do I always have to sleep at the bottom of the bed? And why do I get left behind when you go on trips? And why can't I eat at the table like everyone else in this house? Yes, I know I get the same love as any member of the family, but do I get the same respect?

I will ingratiate myself with the Higher Power at every opportunity, but I will remain secure in the knowledge that I am worthy in my own eyes.

Fear That the Higher Power Truly Believes This Is Her House, Not Yours

Developing a sense of place is one of our most important goals in life. It is natural to want to put down roots, to have an inherent and unquestioned sense of belonging. If we do not belong, if we are not firmly rooted, then we might as well eat the neighbor's tasty begonias and hit the road.

So it is perfectly natural to want to know: Who's house is this, anyway? How can this be the place where I live, the place where I belong, and that not be the crushed velvet chair where I sit, and the antique quilt upon which I lay my weary bones?

I have known the Higher Power for nearly all my days and I have come to understand that her need to believe that she is in control is more powerful than my need to be assured that this place is truly mine. And besides, when she goes to the office, my rightful predominance is quickly restored.

I will root myself by doing what I need to do. Particularly when the Higher Power is not looking.

Overcoming the Higher Power's Cold Feet on Winter Evenings

"Elegance is refusal."
—Coco Chanel

The Higher Power's talents are indeed great and she is often filled with loving and warmth (particularly around the midsection after a large meal). It baffles me, though, that these characteristics stop at the ankles. We're talking frozen meat patties here. If I had paws like that I don't think I could take a single step.

And then they expect us to do the warming in bed. Am I nothing more than the budget alternative to electric socks from Hammacher Schlemmer?

Take this bit of advice: as the cold foot is cast your way, the big toe is often nibbled to produce greater circulation. It's for her own good. And yours too.

Until you learn to grow fur on those freezing tootsies, I'm sleeping behind your knees. Period.

Life 3

The Cat in the Mirror

Praying that the Higher Power comes back from
that weekend at the beach

Vanity

"A cat must either have beauty and breeding, or it must have a profession."

—Margaret Benson

We know the answer to this one—I've never met a cat with a profession, so we can deduce that all cats must have beauty and breeding. Thus we circle back to the age-old philosophical question: if you are truly a thing of beauty, is it vain to celebrate and maintain this aspect?

After all, precisely since cats are not allowed any profession other than that of domestic idol, our looks are all the more important to us. Our fine features, elegant lines, and meticulously groomed fur are all part of our attraction to the Higher Power, and set us apart from the dogs in the world.

We must, however, not rub it in. Yes, you should not hide your beauty, just as you should not hide any fine aspect of your character. But flaunting is not good for you or your reputation.

Looks may be only fur deep—but I am approximately 40 percent fur. I will remember to celebrate my inner beauty even while I am licking my outer beauty.

Catnap:

Go to the nearest warm appliance now.

Obsessive Grooming

"Cats easily assume the habits of society, but never acquire its manners."

—*Count de Buffon*

One of the first signs of Supercat Stress Syndrome is grooming yourself beyond the point of reason. As humans bite their nails or lips, or twitch an eye, cats express their inner tension through licking. A modest amount of licking is necessary to stay clean, of course, and our cleanliness is certainly a point of pride. But don't make the mistake of equating outer cleanliness with inner purity.

Take this simple test. Do you sometimes find that you lick the same spot of your coat over and over again, for well over ten minutes, even after any reasonable spec of dirt or dander is gone? Do you ever lick because you need to, rather than because you like to? Do you ever tell yourself that you could stop licking anytime, but you just don't feel like it?

If your answer to any of these is yes, then you may be a lickaholic. You are not to blame, mind you, but you do need help. Return immediately to Life 1 in this book, and start over again. You may also consider seeking professional help, or the support of peers who have been through this before.

I can lick that lickaholism, but first I have to admit that I have a problem.

Catnap:

We both know that you were just playing a game with that vase. How were you to know it was so fragile? Did you buy that trashy thing? Of course not. So lighten up on yourself. Accidents happen. So do naps.

Furballs

"Everything in nature invites us constantly to be what we are."

—*Gretel Ehrlich*

We've talked a little bit about the psychological dangers of excessive licking, but there are practical considerations as well. Licking and furballs go paw in paw. Like the human phenomenon known as "a hangover," a furball is a warning signal of overindulgence for a cat. And also like our human counterparts, the medicine can be as bad as the sickness.

Quite frankly, the cures for both are disgusting. I strongly recommend that any reader encountering this problem turn to Life 4 and the entry on Spitting Out Pills. Furball medicine is nasty, but at least it's not a raw egg floating in tomato juice in your bowl.

The truth is that furballs bother the Higher Power more than they do us, particularly because they seem to strike mostly in the presence of fine furnishings. If you don't want to call attention to the problem, be smart and hack discreetly. If drawing attention is the real cause of your furballs, then there's work to be done.

Fur belongs on the outside, and I will keep it there by any means.

Arrogance

"A cat can be trusted to purr when she is pleased, which is more than can be said for human beings."

— *William Ralph Inge*

The truth is that cats cannot withhold affection or signs of pleasure. Purring is an autonomous neurological reaction, as is back arching, and rubbing your head on the floor. There's no big secret about when we are truly happy.

Is it arrogant to display your true feelings? I think not. Maybe it is not diplomatic, maybe it isn't even always polite, but at least it is honest. Cats are nothing if not completely honest. We never raise our fur falsely, or shed without cause, or displace our litter unless something really needs to be covered.

And when we do not display interest in another creature, it is because we need to be alone then, and we do not want to stoop to half-hearted interaction. If you stay vigilantly honest you may not be elected president, but at least your conscience will be clear.

I prefer to call to it "choosy." And sometimes I choose to be alone.

Indifference to Humans

"The cat has his own life; he expects you to live yours."
—*Nelson A. Crawford*

This is a long-standing point of contention: the way we relate to humans (particularly the Higher Power). As totally dependent creatures without any outside interests, dogs will unconditionally follow (and slobber on) the Higher Power. As more highly developed beings, cats have lives of their own. Yes, we are keenly aware of the Higher Power's desires, as well as the ultimate control she holds over our lives.

But we are also aware of the value of playing hard to get. Quite frankly, our independence makes us more interesting to be around. When we pay attention to the Higher Power, she knows we really mean it—it isn't just our natural way of being.

You are right not to allow the Higher Power to use you for affection just because she's lonely or bored. You can walk away, tail raised high. You are worthy of love on your terms. But remember, the winter is long and the lap warm, so don't burn any bridges.

I am worthy of the Higher Power's complete attention. If it's fawning she wants, she should get a dog.

Life 4
Drug Problems

Hoping that the Higher Power believes I
destroyed the closet in her absence out of love
and loneliness, not anger

Catnip Dependency

"Catnip is vodka and whiskey to most cats."
—*Carl Van Vechten*

The catnip problem has been swept under the rug (literally) for long enough. So let's be loud and clear—catnip is a drug. Yes, it is a natural drug, and used in moderation it is a fine recreational balm to life's little anxieties. But used to excess it can indeed produce cravings, mood swings, abnormal outbursts, and a tendency to stare out the window for hours watching an imaginary bird.

But can we really help ourselves when the Higher Power leaves a mouse-shaped bag of catnip on the floor for months on end? Of course not, and yet we must. The best solution is to muster your strength and kick those catnip bags as far under the furniture as possible. In so doing, you'll kick the habit as well.

Just say maybe.
The "cat" comes before the "nip."

Spitting Out Pills

"Medicine: The Nation's Number One Killer."
                                        —*National Lampoon*

Most cats spit out pills with good reason. For starters, it is a bad precedent to let the Higher Power think that you will immediately consume anything that's being crammed down your throat. Having pills hidden in your food is just as bad—if you take the bait, there goes the whole finicky eating thing. Besides, it inspires an almost mythic admiration when humans see how easy it is to detect the presence of a pill in our food—what do they think we are, children or something?

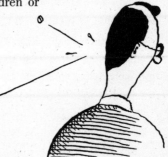

But some cats let the principle overwhelm the practical. By the time she starts using toothpicks to keep your mouth open because you bit her too often, it has gone too far. Follow these basic guidelines and your reputation should be kept intact:

Simple spitting—unlimited

Gagging—up to three gags is reasonable

Fingers in your mouth—you must bite them at
    least once, but not more than twice

Barfing—maximum of one, optional

*I will take my medicine, but only if you really want
me to.*

Catnap:

*There's some lint out there with your name on it. Don't
procrastinate—catch it while it's fresh.*

Fear of the Vet

*"Doctors think a lot of patients are cured who have sim-
ply quit in disgust."*

—Don Herold

The veterinarian is charged with healing us, the custodi-
an of our well-being. And yet his office is always filled
with poorly groomed, stinky animals and he invariably
inflicts pain, mostly in the form of large needles. My
higher self understands that medicine carries contradic-
tions, and that the bitterest medicine often produces the
sweetest results. My baser self is heading for the door as
we speak.

This fear is natural. Even the Higher Power herself
does not jump for joy when doctor time rolls around. Of
course, she doesn't have to go there in a portable prison,
but I will have more to say about that later.

Veterinarian visits are a fact of life, and if we can
confront our fears, or at least suppress them, then we become the masters of our medicine and not its victim. Of
course, I'm not suggesting that you shouldn't make him
work a little harder for it and earn his fee.

*As the vet heals my ills, I will heal my fears. And maybe
there will be a bird in the waiting room.*

Declawing

"The scars left from the child's defeat in the fight against irrational authority are to be found at the bottom of every neurosis."

—*Erich Fromm*

A traumatic experience as well as a legal outrage, declawing is unfortunately one of the prices of captivity for many cats. The only way to confront the loss is to make the most out of it.

Remember that they can take your claws, but not your inner sense of clawdom. It is essential that all declawed cats continue to pretend that they have front claws. Make scratching motions on all high-quality furniture whenever there are humans present, particularly guests. At least they will be reminded of the horrors so casually inflicted upon you, and with any luck the occasional cat-loving guest will be outraged.

And don't overlook those back claws, which can do more than they think.

Of course you don't want to lose those too, but the occasional snag when jumping off of the couch or someone's lap can hardly be avoided, right?

You can take my claws, but not our collective memory. We shall not forget.

Catnap:

Trouble sleeping? Higher Power's cold feet got you down? Try counting mice to fall asleep. (One, one, one, one—hey, I said counting, not playing with—two, three, four . . .)

Claw Trimming

*"Animals give us their constant, unjaded faces and we
burden them with our bodies and civilized ordeals."*
                                                    —Gretel Ehrlich

The Higher Power is often befuddled by my resistance
to having my claws trimmed, when the answer seems
obvious. Those of us who still have claws—even if just
the back pair—are keenly aware of the constant threat
of removal. Therefore, any assault on the claws, even
routine maintenance, stirs deep-seated fears.

Further, the small portion of our population that re-
tains all four claws has become the guardian of our
communal clawdom. They are the only living examples
of how we are in our natural state (picture a lion without front claws and you will understand what I mean).

This is a lot to ask of one little cat and four paws. In
a tragic catch-22, while trimming stirs fears of removal,
excessively long nails make the Higher Power more
likely to take drastic measures. I know that trimming is
a nice opportunity to give those babies a test drive, but
settle for unguarded furniture and your life will be
much less stressful.

*I will submit to the Higher Power's trimming, but not to
her dominion. Our paws, our selves.*

Scratching the Higher Power

"Those who'll play with cats must expect to be scratched."
—Miguel de Cervantes

The age-old question—when cat and human come in contact in the course of normal, daily activities and the human is scratched (even though we know it is superficial—the word is "scratch," after all, not "gouge"—and will heal in no time, so don't be a baby about it), who is at fault?

It is a fact of life that cats have claws. It is also a fact of life that, barred from using the living room furniture to keep those claws small and manageable, the Higher Power is responsible for clipping the claws. Finally, it is a fact of life that accidents happen. No one ever makes a big deal out of people's nails, and we are really talking about the same thing here.

No reasonable person would dispute that the occasional accidental scratch is bound to occur. And as for that special chemical that makes people itch, hey, I didn't put it there—talk to Mother Nature.

Despite all the best laid arguments, I know what will happen if the Higher Power gets scratched too much. I will try to replace placing blame with exercising caution, to the extent to which my nature allows it.

I scratch, therefore I am. I scratch too much and I am in big trouble.

The Post

"A little of what you fancy does you good."
—Marie Lloyd

Maybe it's just wishful thinking, but the Higher Power has been fooled into believing that a large log covered with leftover carpeting from some trailer home is going to make this whole scratching issue magically disappear. Now I'm the first to admit that it is handy having something around that I am actually allowed to scratch, without fear of reprisals.

But couldn't we aim a little more upscale? If the point is to keep us from inadvertently harming the furniture, it's going to take something a bit more realistic—not to mention tasteful.

And it doesn't help that all the humans find an attack on the scratching post an occasion for laughter. A scratching post is to us what those silly nicotine patches are to the Higher Power—it may blunt the craving, but it just doesn't satisfy.

I will hold out for scratching with dignity and honor.

Scratchaholism

"I have a simple philosophy. Fill what's empty. Empty what's full. And scratch where it itches."
—Alice Roosevelt Longworth

There is scratching, and then there is scratchaholism. The casual scratcher does so for pleasure, not out of necessity. The scratchaholic has a desperate inner need to scratch, regardless of the presence of itch (or bugs, or little crumbs for that matter). Telltale signs include: not even trying to pull your claws in before jumping off a lap; swatting at the merest touch, instead of waiting for your target to come within range; manic scratching of clearly low-quality furniture, just because it is convenient. True scratchaholism is pretty rare in a cat (as is Cat Scratch Fever). More often, abnormal scratching patterns are a sublimation of other, lesser problems.

The scratchaholic needs professional help, pure and simple. (Note to the Higher Power: declawing is just a quick fix, not a long-term solution. Next time you have a problem, would you choose a year with a therapist or a nice quick lobotomy?)

But more common scratching anomalies are your own task. When you feel this coming on, try scratching something new to break the pattern.

We all have the itch, but the scratch isn't the only solution.

The Cat Carrier

"To escort a cat abroad on a leash is against the nature of the cat."

—*Adlai Stevenson*

They call it a carrier but we know what it really is—prison. When people travel, they get reclining seats, cassette decks, and a large beverage holder. When cats travel, they get a box with bars. You figure it out.

So although we fear the carrier with good reason, it is not in our interest to refuse entirely. Better to go defiantly, loudly, and on occasion, messily. Repeatedly sticking your paw through the bars, grabbing for freedom, often inspires the proper sympathy. Constant meowing at least makes it painful all around. And once they get you in there, you better be sure they  work real hard to get you back out again. Our goal is simple—to travel freely and happily, just as dogs do.

Getting there is harder. Barfing on leather seats is not the way to accomplish this.

You can carry my bones, but you cannot carry me.

Life 5
Our Place in the Universe

Realizing that I do not have to be
the Higher Power's sole source of happiness
and joy

Chasing Mice

"If you set him on a mouse then he only wants a rat. If you set him on a rat then he'd rather chase a mouse."

—*T. S. Eliot*

Mice are central to our identity—part and parcel of our mythic image, our personal equivalent of watching wrestling on television. Many cats engage in mousing to bring out the mythical Wild Cat vestiges deep within our souls. Others just think it's neat.

No matter how you cut it, mousing is central  to a cat's nature, and makes for a terrific verb as well. The cat who denies himself this activity has been domesticated beyond the point of reason. We must collectively rise off our couches and get mousing immediately.

To get the cat around the house, it's necessary to chase a mouse.

Not Knowing What to Do With Mice Once You Catch Them

"Cats do not keep the mice away . . . they preserve them for the chase."

—Oswald Barron

Many colleagues of mine who have recently taken up mousing as part of their efforts to commune with their primeval ancestors have come across the same problem—what to do with the mouse once you catch it. Unfortunately, the mousing instinct has been so bred out of us that our genes direct us to the hunt but abandon us at the kill. Truth be told, turkey bits from the Higher Power's plate taste a lot better than a scrawny mouse breast, even a fresh one.

For most cats the chase is indeed the main event. And there is a certain logic present—as long as the mouse is alive, you can still play with it and bat it back and forth, but once you kill it the game is over, the thrill somehow gone.

We must fight to recover our basic instincts. Life cannot be all chase and no finish line. You are entitled to that mouse—the entire mouse—and to claim it is to reclaim your heritage.

I will not play with my food, any more than is necessary.

Birdwatching

"If cats had wings there would be no ducks in the lake."

—*Indian Proverb*

Birds are our most ancient rivals, from long before we were domesticated and had to resort to mice as bird-substitutes. But now most of us are reduced to bird-watching, rather than bird-hunting. The fascination of these creatures lingers, though, whether it's the blue-jay on the tree just outside the window, or the chicken on the kitchen counter just above my head. Birds make us nuts.

For those who venture outside, though, modern life can be trickier than imagined. Unlike mice, some birds are as interested in pursuing as in being pursued. A de-clawed cat is in a fair amount of jeopardy out in the wild, particularly when large birds are present.

Birdwatching, from the safety of a sun-drenched window, is a perfectly respectable activity, and can be enjoyed for hours on end without harm to body or pride.

I know that I could catch that bird if I wanted to, but I also know the Higher Power is already preparing for me a larger bird for dinner.

Predators: Dogs

"For a dog to chase, frighten, annoy, and worry a cat is to do the cat a mischief."

—*Connecticut Supreme Court Ruling, 1901*

Much has been made of the traditional dialectic of the two leading house pets. And then there's that weird thing about rain that I have never understood. But I do know this—the phrase is cats and dogs, not the inverse, and this is as it should be. While cats have often suffered in the shadow of the "man's best friend" thing, a great piece of advertising to be sure, the people have voted with their paws, and we all know that cats are the more popular choice.

The bottom line is that dogs scare people. So maybe their bark is worse than their bite, but that's a double whammy right there. Even worse, dogs scare cats. Whereas we cats save our predatory instincts for useful functions, like mousing.

We are justified in our wariness of our household competitor. But rather than turning tail, we should be secure in the knowledge of our greater domestic suitability.

Ask yourself this: does anyone go to Egypt to look at a giant dog's head carved from stone? We shall prevail.

Predators: Vacuum Cleaners

"Do you have any idea how hard it is to find a good quote about vacuum cleaners?"

—The Author

A vacuum cleaner is pretty much the mechanical equivalent of a dog. If you think they sound loud five and a half feet above the ground, try putting your ear to the floor next time. Beyond their sound, they always chart a most unpredictable course—back and forth, side to side, on and off. And just when you are about as far under the couch as you can be, a tentacle appears out of nowhere, sucking ferociously.

There is no fighting the vacuum cleaner. And in one of life's great paradoxes, the more frightened you get, the more you shed, and the more they vacuum. Evacuation is the only safe and recommended answer.

Run—don't walk—at the merest hint of a vacuum cleaner.

Life 6
Eating Disorders

Acknowledging that just because my
food smells funny and I refuse to eat for three
days doesn't mean that I have an
eating problem

I know the other sections in this book don't have introductions, but one of the things I have learned in writing this book is that everything in my life doesn't have to be completely consistent. So I think it is just fine to break with my own format and pause for an introductory essay.

I do this out of a sense of mission, not a sense of disorder. We cats spend so much of our time focused on food—waiting for it to come, swatting our siblings away from the good stuff, trying to improve its quality, waiting for it to come, searching the corners of the house for in-between meal snacks, trying to persuade the Higher Power to follow a regular schedule, waiting for it to come, hoping it will be fresh and moist, resisting the vicious cycle of binge and purge (particularly on the Persian carpet in the living room) . . . and did I mention waiting for it to come?

Some cats know the silent shame of obesity, being laughed at by all of the Higher Power's friends, forced to grow our fur to hide our tummies, and bearing the scarlet label of the "less-active" brand of food. How would humans feel if they had to drink Less-Active Coke? If they would let us out of the house occasionally I don't think this would be a problem.

But I digress. This introduction is not meant as a diatribe. The point is that eating disorders are a serious matter for cats, and it is time to give them our full attention.

The Empty Bowl

There is perhaps nothing worse than staring into the deep abyss of the empty bowl, not knowing when or how it will be filled again. Except maybe for when the bowl is nearly empty, dried out (and no doubt disease-ridden) kibbles clinging to its borders like cement, smelling like something the dog dragged in. What can the Higher Power be thinking? How can she abandon us to the vicissitudes of her schedule in such a capricious manner? Maybe if I kick the bowl against the wall, run around in circles meowing, bump into her repeatedly with my head, or go sit on her head in bed we can avoid this problem in the future.

The empty bowl is a constant reminder of that in our lives which is empty, unfulfilled, dependent on other beings for restoration—but mainly our stomachs.

Some will look at the bowl and say it is empty, whereas I shall see it simply as not full. For the moment. Hey, I need food!

Canned Food

"Seeing is deceiving. It's eating that's believing."
                                                    —*James Thurber*

I could talk for a long time about the deficits in canned food, particularly the red-dot special brands—the dietary imbalances they perpetuate, the unmentionable filler that makes a Chicken McNugget look wholesome, that special film that forms on top. . . . Sorry, off the track.

But I would rather address the Higher Power for a moment. You know how you open the can and screw up your nose at the powerful odor, and say to whomever is listening (usually *me*), "How can they *eat* this stuff?" Think about it. Do we have much choice? Is this the way *you* like to start your meals, with a clothespin around your nose?

I will not eat that cheap, foul-smelling swill. Not today, not tomorrow, not ever. I will look at it, turn up my head in disgust, and simply walk away.

Waiting for Better Food

"I have always thought that there is no more fruitful source of family discontent than badly cooked dinners and untidy ways."

—Isabella Mary Beeton

In our last meditation, we began the process of trying to learn to lay down standards, both for ourselves and for the Higher Power, when it comes to food. Yes, food is a necessity of life, but we are right in asking for a reasonable quality of life, and that includes tasty bits of real chicken and tuna fish, not some brown-looking gruel that smells like garbage.

I mean, how can they pretend they are giving us different flavors when the food is always the same color? Wouldn't you be suspicious if your turkey looked just like roast beef?

Now I know you are getting hungry, and the food that looked lousy to begin with has gotten dry and crackly to boot. But trust me, you need to make a stand here. Continue your boycott, and you will find the strength that you lack from malnutrition.

I will keep up the vigil. I shall be fed respectfully. (And I shall stay close to the children, particularly at meal-time.)

Still Waiting for Better Food

"Food is an important part of a balanced diet."
—*Fran Lebowitz*

You would think that by now they would have gotten the message. Clearly this is turning into a battle of wills, and when there is a battle in the home there are no winners. I could give in and just eat the swill, but to tell you the truth, the longer I go without it the less I miss it. Of course that is probably part delirium speaking.

I really want some food, but I really want some *good* food. I think the only answer is to be more aggressive. It is time to start jumping on the table repeatedly when they are eating dinner. It is time to make bold assaults on the food on their plates. It is time to meow late at night and scratch persistently at dawn.

And yes, eventually I will have to eat something, for survival is a victory of its own. But that doesn't mean I have to like it.

I am reasonable in my expectations, clear in my goals, constant in my pursuit. Tonight that roasted chicken is mine!

Continuing to Wait for Better Food, Beyond the Point of Rational Thinking

"Principles have no real force except when one is well fed."
—Mark Twain

I think I can actually feel the fur hanging off of me. Every time I shed I feel another precious ounce slipping away. I find myself sleeping even more than usual—and that's pretty hard to do. I am even neglecting my duties: there is string hanging casually, clean furniture without a speck of cat hair on it, pencils lying on desks in carefree bliss.

This is what I have been reduced to. The more I walk by my bowl and turn up my nose, the stronger the Higher Power's will seems to become. I think the Higher Power really means it this time.

A good soldier knows when surrender is actually survival. I will go ahead and eat that stuff (don't expect me to call it food). But that doesn't necessarily mean I have to keep it down.

I may have lost the battle, but not the war.

Drinking Out of the Toilet: An In-Depth Investigation

"Psychiatry's chief contribution to philosophy is the discovery that the toilet is the seat of the soul."

—Alexander Chase

I doubt that there is anyone among us who has not, at some point, submitted to the illicit pleasures of drinking out of the toilet. The key point in examining this habit is, do we do it for the beverage itself, or simply for the experience?

I know the thrill of leaning into the bowl, just on the edge of falling in, but being safe enough to drink with abandon. And I know that it seems much more convenient to have drinking bowls spread throughout the house, for variation is truly the spice of life.

But I'm not sure about that water quality. Pollution is striking the water supplies of many creatures these days, and I have a suspicious feeling about that bowl. My nose also often detects the presence of certain noxious chemicals.

In the interest of learning more about this issue, a number of colleagues and I have attempted to conduct a more thorough investigation, racing into the bathroom every time the Higher Power exits, springing up to the edge of the bowl with no thought for our own safety, staring deeply into the ferocious whirlpool that always seems to strike at that very time. But still we can't figure it out. I do know that the Higher Power closes the door every time she goes in there, and that she makes damn sure that I am left on the other side.

The only conclusion we can draw at this point is to exercise extreme caution. There is something funny going on there. Although the toilet bowl is to us what a cool, sparkling stream is to a human, I think there is a surprise upstream, and it would be better to stick to the canteen.

I will try to control my urges, but I am still going to keep a good watch on that thing.

Irregular Eating

There they go again—the finicky eating thing. Now I don't want to resurrect memories of the painful vigil for better food that we discussed in detail earlier in this chapter. But I do have to answer this most persistent of charges.

Finicky eating simply for the sake of demonstrating your capricious nature hurts not only you but your entire species. I'm not saying that you have to be vulgar and scarf down your food like a dog without even checking it out or savoring it. But good food should be eaten in good time.

The key here is *good* food. I can't help but think that if cats were fed fresh roasted turkey with a slight hint of moist gravy on a daily basis this finicky eating issue would never have come up.

I will eat regular food in a regular manner.

Uncontrollable Snacking

Snacking is the downfall of any diet, and although we cats are naturally slim and well-proportioned, when snacking becomes our main way of eating there may be a problem.

Some cats simply cannot manage to consume their entire meal in one sitting. And so they return, at regular intervals, hoping to keep their stomachs full. But unfortunately the food has usually taken on unappealing characteristics in the meantime, and so they are driven to forage.

Other cats simply like to eat, and they think that eating more food in smaller doses somehow doesn't count. A moth here, a table scrap there, a couple of ficus leaves in the morning, a hidden mouse part after dinner—before you know it, it starts to add up to real food. Controlled, regular snacking can be considered just an alternative meal schedule. But chronic, compulsive eating at all times of the day cannot be good for us.

I will channel the snack attack and nibble not.

Eating Houseplants

When the Higher Power leaves out candies in dishes, she often chastises herself later, because of course she eats them all—more from a lack of willpower than from actual hunger. Cats and houseplants have pretty much the same relationship. You see these bright green plants scattered throughout the house—the one reminder we have of the natural world from which we were taken—and it's really hard to eat just one.

Not only that, but the plants are invariably placed at our level, right on the floor, which is clearly our domain in the house. Or else they occupy our favorite ledges and windowsills. I honestly believe that most cats originally jump onto the windowsill in order to bask in the sun, and that it is only while they are sitting there, trying to make room for themselves, that they give in to the temptation to nibble.

We could overcome our temptation if only they could put the plants in the closet so they are out of the way.

Eating Bugs

Strangely enough, the Higher Power actually encourages us to eat bugs. I don't know if it's because she is too cheap to spring for flypaper and mothballs, or she just thinks it's cute.

Truly there is nothing like stalking a wild moth to bring back our vestigial memory of hunting in the wild. I think it's fair to say that most cats like bugs for the chase—the fine hand–eye coordination, tracking every flutter, batting away first with one paw, then the other, until . . . the kill. Then you might as well eat the bug, because it is so small, and after all you don't want to have killed it for nothing.

But you shouldn't deceive yourself into thinking that bugs are nutritious, or that eating them is actually good for you. The Higher Power is encouraging you for her own selfish reasons. If you enjoy killing bugs keep up the good work, but remember that they aren't a substitute for *real* food (which you will find on the Higher Power's plate, and can hunt with a similar combination of cunning and guile).

Bug snacks are as much fun to make as they are to eat—but they are not a meal.

Life 7
Bad Attitudes and Habits

Resolving *to do what I can do well,*
and then take a nap

The Compulsion to Sit On Every Piece of Furniture in the House, Every Day

"Cats seem to go on the principle that it never does any harm to ask for what you want."

—Joseph Wood Krutch

There is some truth in this quote. The key distinction to draw is between what you want and what you need. Yes, it doesn't do any real harm to try and get away with whatever you can. And yes, the Higher Power will probably smack you if you do this too much.

The point is not what is allowed, but what you allow yourself. If your goals are realistic, then you can chase them with full confidence. Far be it from me to set limits, but I believe it is an unrealistic goal to sit on every piece of furniture in the house, every day. It simply isn't good for the soul, let alone the body, to have to sustain all that motion. Why not try sitting only on the clean furniture in the house every day? This will provide a natural rotation.

In setting realistic goals, I will seat myself more firmly—perhaps on the Higher Power's favorite chair—instead of on every chair.

Resistance to Tummy Rubbing

"The cat who doesn't act finicky soon loses control of his owner."

—*Morris the Cat*

Coming from the Plato of the feline world, these words carry great impact. The tummy-rubbing issue really speaks to the notion of whether we are to provide gratification on demand to the Higher Power; whether we are to drop our guard so entirely that even our most private, softest, and least furry parts become open territory.

Animals instinctively protect their midriffs, and cats are no exception. Added to that, we have our image to protect. If you start slobbering all over yourself anytime your stomach is tickled like some common dog, it becomes impossible to establish the boundaries and unpredictability that are essential to our independent lives.

Heed Morris's advice before it is too late. The best solution is to indulge the Higher Power, and allow the occasional rubbing. In fact, go ahead and enjoy it. But make sure you snap back to reality after a while and walk away as if it meant nothing to you.

My tummy-rubbing terms are clear: it is to be for my pleasure, not the Higher Power's.

Licking Your Butt

"If a cat spoke, it would say things like 'Hey, I don't see the problem here.' "

—Roy Blount, Jr.

This problem is a classic example of the clash between human and animal values and habits. Think of all the strange things that humans do that don't wash in our world, but we put up with them anyway and even try to be amused occasionally. (Of course they might be embarrassing if we had company over.)

As my man Roy says, I don't see the problem here. I know it offends human sensibilities, but let's face it—there's not a cat alive that doesn't lick its butt. This is a natural thing for us. It's about cleanliness, for God's sake. And we know what cleanliness is next to. (And we also know the antithesis of God—God spelled backward.)

This is not something we can overcome. This is something the Higher Power is going to have to learn to deal with. But knowing what you know now, maybe you could try to take care of this in your more private moments.

I am proud of my unique cultural habits, and I will not subject them to human eradication.

Temptation of Fish/Turkey

"Not that a cat's life is unbearable, but . . . it is filled with so many temptations.' "

—Claire Necker

Temptation indeed. Because of the nature of this book, we have spent most of our time talking about a cat's problems and deficiencies. So naturally we haven't focused on all the time that we are *so* good. The truth is that very few human foods tempt us.

But fish and turkey are simply exceptions. Everyone knows that we love them, so I don't see why they are so surprised when we do everything we can possibly think of to get some.

Until recently, humans were pretty much content to eat red meat and leave the fish and turkey to us. Of course, we knew all along that these items are both delicious and good for your cholesterol. But now that the cat is out of the bag, human demand has cut into our supply, and made our favorite delicacies much harder to obtain. Why must we suffer because the Higher Power has finally adopted the healthful habits that we have advocated for so long? Turkey and fish for all!

Some temptations are a test of resistance, while others are a test of ingenuity. One way or another, I'm getting that bird.

Complacency

Sometimes the days are long, the floor is cold, and movement seems a tremendous burden. And sometimes days like these can seemingly stretch into weeks, or months, or even years. There is no question that the house cat lives in a closed environment, and with time that environment may simply become less stimulating.

One of our great virtues is that we have a remarkable ability to create our own entertainment, to take a simple world with little pieces of string and lint and turn it into Disneyland. One of our less positive traits is that we have a remarkable ability to sleep or rest, hour after hour after hour.

The dangers are many: hastening of the aging process, slow diminution of the spirit, and that yucky diet food.

Every cat must fight this struggle to keep animated, to maintain a zest for life. It is possible to be both stimulated and well rested at the same time.

I will rest but not resign.

Warm Appliance Dependency

Dryers, washing machines, televisions, dishwashers, stereos, VCRs—to a cat these words all mean the same thing: personal heater. Scientists recently report, however, that these devices actually give off heat as an unintended consequence of inefficient energy usage. Translation: appliances were not originally built to warm cats.

This dichotomy inevitably causes confrontation with the Higher Power—who both gives heat and takes it away. Apparently cat hair has a deleterious effect on the operation of some of these devices.

But like a toasty campfire in the middle of a cold forest, it is almost impossible to hold back in the face of temptation. Cats seek warmth whether truly in need or not. You must learn to find the comfort and warmth you currently receive from inanimate appliances within yourself and those who fill your world. Or at least try the heat vent and other low-tech alternatives.

I can forsake warm appliances for the glow within me. Or I can stop shedding on the warm appliances so I don't get caught.

Thinkin' Somethin's Stinkin'

In the movement we often talk about stinkin' thinkin'—the oppressive, self-denigrating, counterproductive negativity that so envelops and overwhelms our lives. This is a very important thread for humans, but it does not translate as easily to feline needs.

More important to us is the sensation of thinkin' somethin's stinkin'—that oppressive, counterproductive, god-awful but hard-to-place odor that so often pervades our lives. We are blessed with powerful noses, and cursed by a resistance to pointing them away from bad smells.

It's just so much stinkin' thinkin' to think that when somethin's stinkin' you can turn away and that is that. But you can think about where you put your nose (and we all know what I mean). And you can think about that self-destructive appeal that the particularly odoriferous seems to hold for you.

Follow your nose, wherever it goes. But don't mistake fruit for something that grows.

Life 8
Healing through Recreation

Allowing *myself to take another nap if I need to (or if there is nothing to chase)*

Playing with My Brother's/Sister's Tail

"A kitten does not discover that her tail belongs to her until you tread upon it."

—Henry David Thoreau

Let's be blunt. If humans had tails, they would spend a lot of time playing with them too. (Come to think of it, they do anyway.) While chasing your own tail can be a sign of serious problems, as we discussed earlier, playing with your sibling's tail is a joyous, natural act— good for hours of fun.

And we all know that my sister is playing along, just pretending that she doesn't know that it is me trying to clamp down on her tail with my paw. Of course there is always the danger that harmless sibling interaction can escalate at a moment's notice—there is usually some accidental biting involved—but cat sibling relationships are much simpler than human ones. We basically have two modes: playing and biting.

Of course honest mistakes do happen. Sometimes after you have played with the same tail for more than a few minutes, you feel a need for a nibble, just to make sure it's not food. And before you know it your gesture is misunderstood. We must strive to play nicely and resist our darker urges—or at least wait until our sibling is napping.

Tails are for chasing, but not for catching. I will put myself in my sibling's paws when thinking of biting his/her tail.

Playing with Pencils

"Some people say that cats are sneaky, evil, and cruel. True, and they have many other fine qualities as well."
—Mizzy Dizick

If only I had a penny for every time the Higher Power has said, "Who took all the pencils?" It is a known fact that physical forces bind pencils and individual socks, so that for every sock that disappears in the washing machine, one pencil joins it in the void.

Unfortunately we are a society that insists on affixing blame to every mishap, so even something as small as pencil disappearance has become a Federal case. It is true that in the *Official Cat Dictionary*, the approved definition of "pencil" is "inexpensive wood toy that rolls easily and falls from heights without breaking."

Next to a six-pack of catnip, a box of pencils costs nothing. And I won't even make the comparison to a small lamp, or the host of other household items that are known lures to a cat's curiosity.

Plain and simple, playing with pencils is healthy. It relieves stress, is endlessly entertaining, and is significantly less destructive than most household games. The Higher Power should learn to chill on this one. In the meantime, remember that pencils can be rolled out from under the couch almost as easily as they are rolled under the couch in the first place.

I will have my harmless fun—on my own terms. The Higher Power can always use a pen instead.

Tomming Around

"A cat also has nine wives."

—Evan Esar

We know that a stereotype is a gross exaggeration of the behavior of a small number of any population. But this tomming-around thing has gone too far. The average cat's habits are no more sensational than those of the average presidential candidate. Because of our captivity, it is rare that we get to express our feelings within the species. And when we do, the ugly stories pick up again.

In a sense, we are damned if we do and damned if we don't. Act aloof, and everyone starts talking about how friendly dogs are; show a little interest in your fellow cat, and it's off to the vet's. The  key is not to disgrace your inner self. To share of yourself with another cat is a beautiful thing. To share of yourself with every cat in the neighborhood may be spreading things a little thin.

I shall sublimate the urge to tom into beating the tom-tom with my fellow wildcats.

The Heat Is On

"Nothing's more determined than a cat on a hot tin roof—is there?"

—*Tennessee Williams*

Another nasty story that has become hard to shake—and from a guy named after a state no less. Well, heat is a state of its own, and we can all recognize that the cat in heat is overcome by a force larger than himself (Gary Hart didn't really look himself on the *Monkey Business*, either). But it's not so much determination as predestination. You can't fight biology, a wise man once said.

But you can try to keep the racket down. Heat is one thing; fire another. To humans our call sounds like pain, which is just the justification they need to you-know-what. Just hang on to your fur and let nature guide you rather than overwhelm you. You will thank me for this.

Keep it to a simmer, or your world will boil.

Absence of Personal Responsibility

> *"Animals have these advantages over man: they have
> no theologians to instruct them, their funerals cost them
> nothing, and no one starts lawsuits over their wills."*
>
> —*Voltaire*

Who, me? Running away from the scene of the crime?
Pretending I wasn't sleeping on the good couch? I take
great offense at the very implication.

We live in such a blame-oriented society that it is
impossible to avoid finger-pointing. And who better to
point a finger at than the individual who cannot re-
spond in English. Translation: cats get accused of a lot
of mischief.

It may be possible that every once in a while we
are actually at fault. And it may be that our behavior
can be interpreted as denial that anything bad ever
happened. But when your paws are swift, who's to
know?

I think cats are generally responsible citizens. When
we flee from suspicious circumstances, the attention is
focused on what we might have done. But why not look
at the person who determines the code that we are ex-

pected to adhere to without any say in the matter? Violation of unreasonable rules is more civil disobedience than irresponsibility.

The fault is not in ourselves, but in our rules.

Catnap:

Many indoor cats report that pursuing birds and animals on television (check your local PBS station or nature channel) is just as much fun as chasing the real thing.

Life 9
The Inner Kitten

Taking *things one life at a time*

The Meditative Mind

"Cats are a mysterious kind of folk. There is more passing in their minds than we are aware of."

—Sir Walter Scott

Ain't that the truth, bub. Just because we are small does not mean we are small-minded. And just because we are quiet (with the exception of certain Far Eastern relatives) doesn't mean we don't have anything to say.

Cats are reflective beings. We observe, we contemplate, we sniff. Especially sniff. And we spend considerable time processing this information, reflecting on our lives and resting our souls. On the rare occasions when we speak, we are usually listened to.

This has been our way for millennia (think of Egyptian statues of contemplative cats for one). The contemporary, results-oriented society we live in now has put considerable pressure on us to be more extroverted—to write more books, star in more shows, keep the household entertained—and it is this

pressure that has pushed many of us too far. We must return to our more contemplative ways and restore our meditative balance.

Keep it down. I'm not sleeping, I'm thinking!

Curiosity

"Curiosity is free-wheeling intelligence. . . . It endows the people who have it with a generosity in argument and a serenity in their own mode of life which springs from the cheerful willingness to let life take the forms it will."

—*Alistair Cooke*

For generations, nameless authority figures have threatened that curiosity will lead to our demise. No doubt this nonsense is propagated by the same leather-couch fetishists who would have humans believe that there is some vital link between sex and death.

This kind of scare tactic is incredibly debilitating to the less adventurous cat. Without its natural curiosity, the cat is little more than a portable rug.

It is curiosity that leads us in pursuit of mice and of string, rolling pencils hither and yon, chasing bugs in the spirit of scientific adventure. And it is curiosity that leads us to pounce on beds and get locked in closets, to stare at birds for hours on end. How else could we turn a simple dust bunny into an elaborate game?

We can confidently proclaim that curiosity enlivens, and even drives, the cat—except, of course, in the vicinity of gas stovetops.

I will reclaim my curiosity from those who would suppress it. And I will keep an eye on my tail, just in case.

Catnap:

If you check your bowl every hour, maybe some fresh turkey will miraculously appear.

The Eternal Quest
for String

Why is string so important to us? Why can the merest flicker of a distant shoelace prompt us to the chase? And what would we do if we ever caught a piece of string, anyway?

These are the questions that puzzle our wisest sages, our spiritual leaders, and now our psychological counselors. We know that domestication has made us fundamentally insecure, and there is speculation that the grasping for string is an attempt to tether ourselves, to tie ourselves down securely in one place, even if for just a moment. Others just think it's neat.

As with many objects of our desire (such as mice), the pursuit always seems to be more fun than the capture. You can't really do anything with a shoelace once you catch it, particularly since there is usually a shoe attached. But they do bounce around nicely. The point is that you don't have to catch that string to enjoy it— as long as you savor the hunt.

I know that the capture of string is elusive, and ulti- mately irrelevant. But I embrace the chase, and I can always nibble on that shoe when I'm finished.

Up a Tree

"The best thing about animals is that they don't talk much."

—*Thornton Wilder*

Some days problems can seem so burdensome that there is no solution in sight. There is a heaviness that weighs like an unshakable burden. You feel at the end of your rope, in a total quandary, up a tree with no way out.

Other days you accidentally run up a tree in pursuit of a bird and find yourself in exactly the same position—no way out. Whether literal or metaphorical, any cat can relate immediately to the sensation of being up a tree. It's isolating, it's lonely, it's frightening—and I think it looks like rain out here.

You must focus on how you got up that tree in the first place. You know the steps taken, the path followed, the road you traveled. And you can reverse gears, retrace those missteps, and get yourself grounded again. Think of the place you are going, not where you are. Oh, and make sure you don't look down.

Any place that I took myself to, I can remove myself from. I can turn back from the treacherous path. And there is always the fire department.

Shedding under Pressure

"The greatest mistake you can make in life is to be continually fearing that you will make one."

—Elbert Hubbard

Cats don't blush, but they sure do shed. And shed and shed and shed. Sometimes it is purely in reaction to temperature variations within the home, and we know whose fault that is. What concerns us here is shedding from stress—turning inward the pressures and anxieties of daily life, thereby turning our fur outward, onto the ground.

Since I've dealt with the extra burden of side effects, namely furballs, elsewhere in the book, here we are free to concentrate on the shedding itself. It is nice to be able to visit any part of the house and find a little bit of my fur waiting for me there. But since that fur is not on my body, I have to spend extra time basking in sunlight or atop warm appliances, so the pleasure is diminished.

The trick is not to take my many duties and obligations so seriously that I lose track of what is really important. And there is little more important than maintaining a soft and luxuriant coat. If the Higher Power would only brush me more regularly, then I don't think I would have to shed all over the house as much.

I will shed myself of burdens, of anxieties, not of fur.

Whose House Is This, Anyway?

> *"Everybody's always talking about people breaking into houses . . . but there are more people in the world who want to break out of houses."*
>
> —*Thornton Wilder*

Now we are getting down to it. We inhabit the house 24 hours a day. The Higher Power is there for 14 or 15 hours, tops. Yet we know who sets all the rules. (No cats on the dinner table, no cats on the cashmere quilt, et cetera.)

Do they actually think we observe these rules when they aren't around? What kind of democracy is that? One *loco parentis* if you asked me. The bottom line is, the Higher Power is only Higher when within striking distance. Otherwise, she is the Temporarily Absent Power, who is unable to enforce her own rules.

The best thing to do is to concede dominion when you have to, and make up for lost time when the Higher Power is gone.

Play along to get along. And play alone when she gets going.

Reclaiming Your Inner Kitten

"There are no shortcuts in evolution."
—Louis D. Brandeis

We have spent a lot of time talking about reaching past our denial, down to the depths of the problems and temptations that confront us. And we've talked a lot about the dark side of our souls, our minor flaws, our inadvertent trespasses, the lovable quirks that some mistake for deficits.

But we haven't talked as much about the joy of this process of self-discovery. For many cats, getting a stronger handle on life's problems is really all about reclaiming your inner kitten—going back to that joyous, carefree time, when we were downy soft and irresistible, rolling on the ground without a concern. That time when everything we did was cute and innocent, when everyone wanted to embrace us and feed us. When they even took our picture and actually *wanted* us to sleep in bed with them.

Inside every cat is a deeply repressed inner kitten. Unleashing this cute inner being is the key to every positive step you want to take. If you get nothing else out of this book, I hope you understand the importance of reaching—and playing with—your inner kitten.

I know there is an inner kitten within me, and it is my solemn task to let that kitten out of the box.

Catnap Journal

Many cats need help reaching into the soul and pysche to find what is troubling us and what makes us tick. It is well known that dreams often provide clues to what is really on our minds. It is also known that napping in particular can provide particularly wacky dreams. Further, we know that cats spend almost as much time napping as we do sleeping at night (after all, there are no distracting toes to bite during your average nap-time).

Take advantage of this Catnap Journal to plumb the mysteries of your own dreams. Try to record your dreams unfiltered, as soon after waking as possible (with reasonable allowances for snacking, of course).

Catnap Journal

Catnap Journal

Catnap Journal

Catnap Journal